PROMOTING

Communication

In Infants & Young Children

500 Ways to Succeed

Jennifer Quick * Alexandra O'Neal

The Speech Bin

Dedication

In loving memory of Barbara J. Heist, the most extraordinary of moms.
– Jennifer

To my parents for all the love, support, and encouragement they have given. A special thanks to my husband, Steven, for being a constant source of inspiration and strength.
– Alexandra

The Speech Bin, Inc.
1965 Twenty-Fifth Avenue
Vero Beach, Florida 32960
1-800-4-SPEECH

ISBN 0-937857-72-6
Catalog Number 1512

Printed in the United States of America

Table of Contents

Preface

In writing a how-to book about promoting the development of communication skills in young children, our goal was to create a reference for parents and caregivers as well as professionals; therefore, we chose to emphasize the practical information we have found most relevant in our early intervention experiences. Information is general enough for beginners yet sufficiently unique to be worthwhile reading for any early interventionist.

Suggestions are divided into topics frequently encountered and placed in the most appropriate section. Much of the information provided is interrelated. Although suggestions are presented in list form, more detailed explanations are provided when further clarification seemed necessary.

Use the material presented as a guide for developing enjoyable activities within the framework of the family's daily life. Activities are not meant to be used as adult-directed drill and practice.

Often one of the most important steps one can take on behalf of young children with disabilities is to get them connected with local early intervention service providers. A team of professionals can make a significant positive impact on a child's development when they collaborate with caregivers about what is likely to work best for a particular child.

Our hope is you can take some of the ideas from this book and incorporate them into enjoyable activities to make some wonderful memories of your own. No book can contain everything a caregiver or service provider needs to know about promoting communication skills in young children. This book contains the information we wish we could have had when starting our careers in early intervention. We hope it is helpful to you.

About the Authors

Jennifer Quick earned her bachelor's degree from Vanderbilt University and her master's degree from University of Illinois in early childhood special education. She is project coordinator of the Early Education Program for Children with Disabilities at University of Southern Mississippi. Her previous experience includes teaching preschool special education in Atlanta Public Schools and providing early intervention services at both Susan Gray School for Children in Nashville, Tennessee, and Raleigh (MS) Early Intervention Center.

Alexandra O'Neal earned both her bachelor's and master's degrees in speech-language pathology at the University of Southern Mississippi. She holds the American Speech-Language-Hearing Association Certificate of Clinical Competence in speech-language pathology and works at South Central Regional Medical Center in Laurel, Mississippi. She previously worked at Laurel Early Intervention Center, Easter Seal School for Special Children, Mobile Preschool for the Sensory Impaired, and United Cerebral Palsy of Mobile.

Promoting Communication

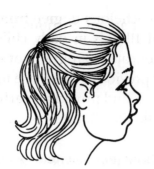

One of the most crucial tools a child can possess is the ability to communicate effectively. Communication development – the development of language and speech – begins at birth. It is greatly influenced by the behaviors of persons who regularly interact with the child.

Early communication begins with the expression of basic emotions and helps establish relationships with caregivers. As language evolves, relationships expand. When a child enters toddlerhood, communication becomes a vehicle for asserting independence. Without an adequate system of communication, children may begin to exhibit behavior problems as a result of their frustration.

As children grow, their social environments continue to expand. Their ability to provide and receive information depends on their previous experiences with communication. All higher learning is based on language. Therefore, early communication skills provide a solid foundation for subsequent learning. As parents, teachers, caregivers, and service providers, you hold so much of a child's future in your hands. How you interact with young children is critical to their development of communication skills.

Before addressing the communication needs of children, individuals must examine their own repertoires of communicative techniques and abilities. Regardless of a person's knowledge and experience, one's skills can always be sharpened. The details of an appropriate intervention situation can and should vary; however, some basic principles always apply. Many, but certainly not all, are described below.

General Information

- Assume changes in a young child's behavior are attempts to communicate. Provide an appropriate verbal expression to accompany the behavior and respond accordingly. For example, if a child begins to squirm or cry when placed in a seat, you might say, "Oh, you're ready to get out," and help the child get out.

- Do something different each day to provide an incentive for communication.

- Encourage children to initiate interactions by setting up situations where they will need to communicate.

Speaking Tips

- Place yourself at the child's eye level when speaking.

- Establish eye contact before communicating. Be sure you have a child's attention by first following the child's eye gaze or pointing, then talking about what you see.

- Slow your speech rate when talking to young children.

- Exaggerate your vocal inflection.

- Be sure to vary your tone of voice while speaking.

- Respond appropriately to the child's tone of voice.

- Use animated facial expressions.

- Be sure your facial expressions match your message.

- Initially pair verbal messages with gestures. Gradually fade or eliminate the gestures as children show greater understanding of what you say.

Topics

- Talk about objects and actions that appear to interest the child.

- Talk about things that are present and concrete rather than remote events.

Language Stimulation Techniques

- Call children by their names often.

- Talk to children – using nouns, verbs, adjectives, and pronouns – throughout all activities. Verbalize what you are doing and what the child is doing as it is happening.

- Reinforce any attempt to communicate.

- Realize overgeneralization is normal for children. For example, a child may initially believe all four-legged animals are dogs. Providing multiple examples of objects can help clarify which fit a certain label.

- Use language one level above the child's level of language usage. For example, if a child is combining two words, respond in three-word phrases or sentences.

- Talk about what you are doing, what the child is doing, and what others nearby are doing while it is taking place.

- Label objects and actions new to the child.

- Provide prompts or cues to allow children to participate in interactions slightly above their current level of ability.

- Whenever possible, offer children choices. First, offer choices between two concrete objects by saying: "Do you want this one or that one?" with the items in view. Later, offer choices between all imaginable possibilities by asking questions such as, "What should we eat today?" When offering children choices, always be sure you can honor their decisions, whatever they may choose. If you cannot, do not offer them a choice.

- Help children use words in their repertoires in a variety of situations.

- Encourage vocalizations and pointing when a child is indicating early preferences.

- Label feelings for children so they will learn the words associated with the emotions.

- Expand on the child's utterances. For example, if a child says, "Look, doggie," respond by saying, "I see the big doggie."

- Encourage children to make requests verbally by modeling the words when necessary.

- Discourage children from overusing "empty words," such as "this," "that," "thing," or "stuff." When they do, model the appropriate words to expand their vocabularies.

- Provide simple commands for children to carry out.

Listening Tips

- Provide ample time for children to respond to questions.

- Be selectively silent when trying to encourage spontaneous communication.

- Show children you are actively listening to them by repeating parts of what they said in your response.

- Pause for turn-taking in conversation.

- Avoid cutting a child's communication short when you disagree. Wait for the child to finish before making your point.

- Provide socially contingent responses. Wait for the child to perform a specific action or make a specific vocalization before you react in a certain way.

- Always provide the least intrusive cues or prompts necessary for a child to respond appropriately.

Responding Appropriately

- Show affection at appropriate times so children will learn to respond in kind.

- Avoid allowing siblings or classmates to talk for children.

- Encourage children to ask for help when needed. If you see they need help and are not asking for it, say, "Do you need help?" and wait for them to respond.

Behavioral Considerations

- Keep your expectations reasonable but high. Always consider a child's individuality above the disability.

- Make every effort to build a child's self-esteem. The more confident children are, the more apt they are to communicate.

- Be negative about a child's specific misbehaviors rather than about the whole child.

- Avoid always anticipating children's needs and being one step ahead of them. Allow them to get hungry, tired, or wet sometimes to provide opportunities for them to communicate their needs.

- Refrain from giving in to children's tantrums.

- Place the blame for miscommunication on yourself instead of placing it on the child.

- Allow children to make mistakes in speech and other behaviors. Avoid overcorrecting them because this may stifle their future communicative attempts.

- Encourage children to participate in age-appropriate activities, providing assistance to them as necessary.

- Break children's expectations periodically, and wait for them to respond.

- Encourage children to be as independent as possible in all situations.

- Permit children to protest when appropriate.

- Shape early communication by selectively assigning meaning to specific behaviors. This is the basis from which all language is learned. For example, responding to the child's utterance "ba" by providing a bottle eventually leads to the child's association of the label with the object.

- Treat children as individuals; avoid comparing them to siblings or peers.

- Use natural rather than artificial consequences and reinforcers. For example, if children break a toy, throw it away so they can no longer play with it instead of hitting, scolding, or otherwise punishing them. Similarly, if a child draws a picture, display it on the refrigerator or in the classroom rather than giving a sticker or other unrelated reward.

- Provide children pets with which they can develop a relationship.

- Arrange for children to have different caregivers. Exposure to different people and different places promotes communication across settings and individuals.

Strictly Physical

- Encourage physical exploration of the environment.

- Make sure children are positioned comfortably before attempting to communicate with them. Positive communication will take a back seat when a child is not comfortable.

- Signing, when paired with verbal messages, will not hurt any child. This will often increase attempts to communicate.

- Be sure you are at the child's eye level before attempting communication.

Social Considerations

- Encourage others to interact with the child.

- Always make sure a child is introduced to everyone present.

- Allow children to interact with their peers as often as possible.

- Help children relax in new social situations. Comfort, rather than pressure, builds the confidence necessary for successful interactions.

Cautions

- If a child has never babbled or stops acquiring new sounds, arrange to have the child checked for hearing problems as soon as possible.

- Have all ear infections treated promptly.

Suggestions for Professionals

- If you are a service provider who sees children individually, try to overlap sessions for a few minutes to provide opportunities for peer interaction.

- Make sure communication is incorporated into all activities and not confined only to a specific instructional time.

Last But Not Least...

- *Relax.* Just enjoy the time you spend with children without always having an intervention agenda.

Talking Through Routines

Establishing routines with infants and young children is very important. Their initial learning is based on the predictability of daily occurrences. These routines offer invaluable opportunities for learning language as well. The following is a list of possible topics for discussion as you move through your daily routine.

- When your child awakens, talk about opening the blinds, the morning sunshine, and time to "wake up."

- During diapering, talk about smell and feel, using words such as "wet," "stinky," "dry," "clean," and "cold."

- When dressing and undressing children, talk about the temperature and weather, names and colors of garments, and whether they are being put on or taken off.

- While cooking and eating, talk about smells, tastes, and names of the foods.

- When playing, talk about toys and objects in which the child shows interest by naming them and talking about what they do.

- At nap time, talk about the child being sleepy and getting items needed for the nap, such as a blanket or favorite stuffed animal.

- When leaving home, talk about going "bye-bye," doors opening and closing, getting in the car, where you are going, and the passing scenery.

- While watching television programs and videotapes, be engaged with the child. Provide extra information about what you see and hear; comment about what is happening. For example, you might say, "Oh, he put that bowl on his head. That's so silly!"

- While bathing the child, talk about each body part as you wash it, the temperature of the water, the smell of the soap, and being "in/out," "wet/dry," and "dirty/clean."

- At bedtime talk about rocking, going "night-night," and sleeping. Sing a lullaby or read to the child.

- Throughout the day, give the child a role in family activities and chores. Participation and positive contributions, however small, build the child's self-esteem and provide more opportunities for communication.

- Make sure the child's daily routine involves changes as well as continuity and stability. A child needs to know what to expect but also needs to have new experiences about which to communicate.

Sensory Activities

Sensory experiences are the building blocks from which infants and young children construct their earliest thoughts. Direct participation in activities that stimulate their senses provides a concrete frame of reference for related language concepts. Everyone can relate to the power of sensory experiences, such as a certain smell that recalls nursery school or the smell of cookies baking that brings back the feeling of home. Without a sufficient variety of such experiences to draw from, children can be delayed in their development of critical early language concepts. Children with disabilities may be especially vulnerable because of limited mobility and/or sensory impairments.

The following activities are rich in sensory stimulation. With a little imagination, they can be modified to be appropriate for all children. This list is not complete; it is meant to spark your creativity in using play to stimulate the child's senses.

- Mealtimes provide excellent opportunities to encourage sensory explanation. This exploration can be heightened by allowing food play and providing foods of various temperatures, textures, and tastes.

- Although not always convenient, allowing messy play is important for children. They need to have the opportunity to explore a variety of materials fully and freely; such exploration facilitates the development of descriptive language and rich vocabularies. Messy but stimulating activities include:

  - Finger-painting with pudding, shaving cream, lotion, paint, or whipped cream
  - Playing with mud by splashing in mud puddles, squishing mud between toes, or making mud pies
  - Participating in sand-box activities
  - Using gelatin, peanut butter, dough, or pasta to make edible creations

- Create bins or pools that contain different materials in which to play and feel. Possible materials include foam packing "peanuts," shredded paper, sand, or water.

- Young children need to experience the sensation of different textures rubbing against or touching their skin. If a child does not seek such experiences, provide activities that facilitate these experiences. Appropriate activities include gently rubbing a baby's cheeks, face, and hands with different textures during bottle feeding or rubbing an older child's feet and hands with carpet, bristle blocks, fake fur, satin, safe metals, and other materials.

- Almost every activity can be a sensory experience. However, some activities integrate many senses and therefore have a more powerful effect. Here are a few favorites:

    - Engaging in gentle tickling games

    - Playing on a trampoline

    - Hand-feeding animals (safety must be considered)

    - Playing in piles of leaves

    - Making popcorn

    - Banging pots and pans

    - Swinging

    - Going on wagon rides

    - Making light shows with flashlights and other lighted toys in a dark room

    - Playing in a pit of balls

    - Going outdoors in different weather conditions

    - Picking flowers

    - Placing baby in a basket of warm laundry (first making sure any buttons, zippers, and snaps are not hot)

    - Giving bubble bath or massage with scented lotion or fragrant soap

    - Bouncing baby on a waterbed or mattress

All activities should be supervised carefully and conducted safely.

Especially for Infants

You cannot begin too early working on interactions with infants. Certain behaviors can facilitate or hinder early communication. Paying attention to the signals an infant is sending is critical. These signals may include facial expressions, pleasant or unhappy vocalizations, or restlessness. Reacting appropriately helps ensure interactions are enjoyable, meaningful, and motivating. Other important considerations for stimulating infants include:

- Repeat the sounds infants make.

- Imitate the infant's facial expressions.

- Encourage and join vocal play.

- Carry infants face forward so they can see what is happening.

- Establish a routine so an infant can develop expectations about daily events.

- Use massage to aid relaxation and establish eye contact.

- Briefly stop a favorite game or activity and wait for infants to send signals of their desire to continue.

- Avoid laying infants on their backs during feeding; never prop a bottle in the infant's mouth. These behaviors can lead to loss of initiative, increased chance of ear infections, baby-bottle tooth decay, aspiration of the milk, and possible related pneumonia.

- Encourage imitation of simple movements, such as patting, shaking, and banging objects.

- In early communication, allow the use of eye gaze to indicate wants.

- Place the infant on a blanket on the floor with a variety of toys available to stimulate movement, choice-making, and communication.

- Provide a variety of activities to develop the concept of object permanence. Make objects disappear and reappear, using jack-in-the-box toys and playing peek-a-boo. Realizing objects continue to exist when they are not in sight precedes the development of most language concepts.

- If an infant lacks a startle reflex, have hearing checked immediately.

- React to vocalizations consistently and positively. This encourages continued vocal expression.

Allow infants to explore toys with their mouths.

- Change room decorations every few months.

- Always respond to a crying infant.

- Vary the sounds you make after imitating the infant's sounds.

- Feed infants on demand rather than on a fixed schedule. This allows additional opportunities for communication.

- Record voices of familiar people to play for the infant.

- Exaggerate your facial expressions when talking to an infant.

- Provide opportunities for an infant to see and interact with other babies.

- If an infant is premature, keep in mind early delays may be the result of the difference between the baby's due date and the date delivered. Therefore, do not be discouraged if early communication skills develop later than those of same-age peers.

- Allow an infant to turn away when overstimulated. If an infant is premature, you may have to break eye contact during periods of obvious overstimulation.

Emphasizing Early Concepts

A child's early words, other than object labels, are most often based on actions or the most salient features of objects. These words can be introduced and reinforced through specific types of play. Below are several suggestions for activities linked to early words.

- Introduce the word "more" during mealtimes by giving smaller portions.

- Teach the child to wave "bye-bye" when leaving or when others are leaving.

- Wait for the child to raise arms when you say "up" and extend hands.

- Provide the word "down" for children when they are becoming restless in your arms.

- Play spinning, bouncing, and swinging games to introduce words, such as "fast" and "slow," "stop" and "go," and "high" and "low."

- Introduce concept of "all gone" during mealtimes and object permanence activities.

- Provide the word and/or sign for "finished" or "all done" when children lose interest in a game or activity.

- Use "uh-oh" to help children label simple mishaps.

- Introduce pronouns early. For example, teach the child to use words to say "mine!" when someone attempts to grab a toy instead of using physical aggression or surrendering passively.

- Allow "uh-huh" and "uh-uh" for "yes" and "no."

- Teach the child to say "stop!" in situations that require protest.

- Always model "please" and "thank you" at appropriate times when talking to the child and to other people.

- Use the labels "inside" and "outside" when entering and leaving the house or building.

- Teach "on/off" and "over/under/through" with playground equipment and activities.

- Teach "open/shut" with doors, containers, and the "Open and Shut Them" hand game.

- Teach "in/out/on" and "next to/behind/in front of" with figurines and doll houses, barns, or play vehicles or when the child is exploring a large appliance box.

- Teach "bring" and "give me" when using simple commands with children.

- Always greet children after an absence to provide an appropriate model.

- Introduce "play," "eat," and "night-night" during appropriate transition times.

- Label "big" and "little" with similar toys of different sizes or when encountering extremely large or small objects.

- Introduce "back" and "forth" while rocking or swinging the child.

- Provide the word "want" instead of allowing whining and pointing.

- Use "no" or "no-no" to identify misbehavior.

- Teach "on" and "off" with radio, television, and battery-operated toys.

- Relate early action words, such as "shake," "bang," "kick," "pat," "get," and "push" to baby's movements.

- Introduce the words "eat" and "drink" by repeating them for younger children while eating and drinking. Use these words with older children during tea parties or feeding or pretending to feed animals.

- Introduce the concepts and words "same" and "different" by providing two objects that are exactly the same and one that is very different.

- Introduce opposites with simple pictures that clearly illustrate the concepts presented.

- Teach "roll," "catch," "throw," and "kick" during simple ball exchanges.

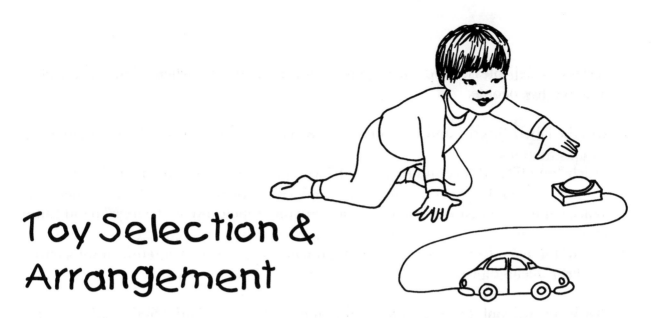

Toy Selection & Arrangement

Types of toys used and the way they are displayed can make an enormous impact on a young child's need and desire to communicate. This is very important aspect of early intervention that is often overlooked. The following suggestions are helpful when purchasing and arranging toys.

- Leave toys in view but out of reach to encourage children to communicate about what they want.

- Talk about a toy when the child shows interest in it. This is more effective than trying to direct the child's attention to a new object.

- Use some toys that talk or have voices.

- Encourage play with toy telephones to elicit vocalizations.

- Record the child's voice and play it for the child to hear.

- Provide a variety of containers that echo when sounds are made into them. Demonstrate.

- Mirrors are popular with children from infancy through the preschool years. Younger children often try to touch and "talk" to the baby in the mirror; older children like to watch themselves while dressing up, dancing, and performing dramatic play activities.

- Provide a variety of toys that perform a consistent action when the child acts on them appropriately to teach the concept of cause and effect. Switch toys are a good option for children with physical limitations.

- Keep bells, rattles, music boxes, and other noisemakers handy for activities to promote auditory localization.

- Make duplicates of family photos so children can have their own copies to play with and communicate about.

- Provide only one set of popular items to encourage sharing and play interactions in group situations.

- Avoid being overly reliant on "high-tech" and battery-operated toys. Children need the reinforcement of their natural environments and encouragement to explore and play with simple items in new and creative ways. Sometimes when children are constantly exposed to the intense stimulation of high-tech toys, they lose interest in interacting when those items are not present.

- Use toys that require two or more participants, such as a rocking boat, a ball, a wagon, walkie-talkies, or simple board games.

- Use toys that incorporate related environmental sounds, such as police cars with sirens and talking toys.

- When doing an activity or giving a snack to children, avoid automatically giving them everything they need or as much as they want. Waiting for them to ask encourages communication.

- Provide props and special areas that encourage dramatic play.

- Make available toys similar enough to provide multiple examples of object categories. For example, provide three different dogs and two different telephones. Multiple examples of like objects help children determine what characteristics make a particular item what it is and not something else. This helps them learn about both overgeneralization and undergeneralization.

- Use puppets to get children involved in stories.

- In classrooms, arrange toys into different centers (such as books, dramatic play, blocks, and table toys) to encourage categorization skills.

- Provide toys that can be used by children who are at many ability levels. Some examples are books, bells, pom-poms, and toy telephones.

- Keep some special items (such as bubbles and stickers) permanently out of sight and out of reach so children must remember their names and ask for these items to get them.

- Provide toys with a variety of possible outcomes (blocks, clay, crayons, and paper) to encourage creative expression.

Environmental Sounds

It is important for children to learn to discriminate, imitate, and identify non-speech sounds in their surroundings. At the most basic level, caregivers can identify sounds as they happen. For example, identify a barking sound by saying, "Listen, the doggie is barking. Woof-woof." Once the child is familiar with sounds and their origins, it is time to work on imitating these environmental sounds during play. At a more advanced level, caregivers can play games with children which include making the sound of an object and encouraging them to name or identify the object by sound alone. Here are some sounds often found in children's environments.

Weather and Seasonal Sounds

- Thunder
- Raindrops
- Leaves crunching
- Wind
- Waves crashing
- Stream gurgling

Animal Sounds (such as farm animals, zoo animals, pets, and insects)

- Lapping
- Slurping
- Barking
- Snorting
- Buzzing
- Purring
- Cock-a-doodle-doing
- Baaing
- Quacking
- Whimpering
- Stomping
- Grunting
- Roaring
- Panting
- Croaking
- Splashing
- Hissing
- Growling
- Squealing
- Pecking
- Chirping
- Mooing
- Neighing
- Oinking
- Howling
- Screeching
- Sniffing
- Whooing
- Meowing
- Chomping
- Rattling
- Scratching

Household Sounds

- Telephone
- Doorbell
- Oven timer
- Alarm clock
- Toilet flushing
- Water running
- Television
- Aquarium bubbling
- Washing machine and dryer
- Popcorn popping
- Knocking
- Door slamming
- Steps creaking
- Radio static

Vehicle Sounds

- Engine starting
- Siren
- Racing gears shifting
- Slamming on brakes
- Ship
- Helicopter
- Beeping alarm used when backing
- Honking
- Motor running
- Airplane
- Train
- Vehicles crashing
- Motorcycle

Human Sounds

- Yawning
- Sneezing
- Humming
- Whining
- Blowing kisses
- Crying
- Sighing
- Gasping
- Teeth chattering
- Snoring
- Coughing
- Laughing
- Babbling
- Whistling
- Smacking lips
- Gulping
- Tongue clicking
- Crunching food

Unusual Sounds

Invent sound effects to accompany specific behaviors; encourage the child to imitate them.

Reading Suggestions

Reading is one of the most important skills a child can acquire to facilitate advanced communication in today's society. Restricting young children from typical prereading experiences simply because they have disabilities is unfair. One need only to consider the example of Helen Keller to be reminded not to underestimate a child's potential abilities. The following suggestions provide opportunities for most children to develop prereading skills; they will not harm any child unless they are taken to the extreme of drill and practice.

- Read to children every day.

- Read stories with repetitive phrases. Encourage children to say these phrases with you each time they occur in the story.

- Use different voices for different characters.

- Read stories with pictures or symbols embedded in the text so children can "read" the pictures, interjecting at appropriate times.

- Encourage children to retell stories and act them out with props.

- Let children predict how stories will end.

- Reread favorite stories over and over and over again.

- Encourage children to learn the names of their favorite characters so they will recognize them in different media and settings (such as toys, books, tee-shirts, and decorations).

- Ask questions at the child's level about stories. Start with "What...?" questions; later move to questions beginning with "Who," "Where," "When," and "Why."

- Label household or classroom objects with cards that have the name or name and picture of the object to which they are attached.

- Write stories about children's experiences exactly as they tell them to you. Encourage children to illustrate these stories. Help them make their own books out of the pages you write.

- Talk about the pictures in storybooks as you read; ask children to point to different pictures as you name them.

- Read stories related to ongoing household and classroom activities.

- Use board books with babies so they can explore them fully without ruining them.

- Use books with attached objects or textures for children to explore.

- Provide some books with photographs, some with full-color illustrations, and some with simple black and white line drawings.

- Make different types of books, such as first words, concept books, and stories, available.

- Use some wordless picture books to encourage children to tell stories.

- Read books related to a child's culture, disability, and familiar activities and problems.

- Place children so they can see the pictures and text as you read. When working with groups or children who have visual impairments, use oversized books or books with large print.

- Sometimes use books with different features, such as pop-up books or books with sound effects or textures.

- Allow a child to choose the book to be read at story time.

- Teach children to recognize common symbols in the community, such as the sign of a fast food restaurant, and encourage them to point these out to you when they see them.

- Provide plenty of reading material for both children and adults. Be sure children are exposed to adults reading for enjoyment and for specific purposes on a regular basis.

- Teach children to identify one or two letters, such as their initials, and encourage them to find these letters in magazines, newspapers, and books.

- Provide children magnetic letters or a small chalkboard and chalk. Ask them to "write" you secret messages. Then, if necessary, ask them to whisper the message to you.

- While shopping, show your child an item on the shopping list and encourage your child to find it on the shelf. For example, say, "Look! This says MILK. Can you get us some milk?" This encourages both communication and the motivation to read.

- Replace a trip to the toy store with a trip to the bookstore. Your child will still have the opportunity to communicate purchase preferences, with the added bonus of developing an appreciation of books and reading.

- Visit the public library to explore books available or attend a storytelling time.

Oral-Motor Exercises

Oral-motor exercises increase the control and function of the oral musculature. This in turn can help improve the intelligibility of speech. Incorporate ideas below into enjoyable activities rather than perform them as drill and practice. The techniques are general enough to be used by anyone with any child without harm. Model the behavior, and encourage the child to imitate.

Lips

- Puff cheeks while keeping lips tightly closed.
- Pucker to kiss.
- Smile.
- Frown, pulling corners of the mouth down.
- Push lollipop with lips.
- Encourage pucker by blowing bubbles, blowing candles, and whistling.

Tongue

- Protrude tongue tip, move it side to side, and try to touch it to nose.
- Lick food from both top and bottom lips.
- Move tongue in a circular motion.
- Push cheek out with tongue.
- Lick lollipop.
- Push lollipop out of mouth with tongue.

Other

- Move air from cheek to cheek.
- Puff cheek, tapping cheek with finger while trying not to let air escape.
- Suck cheeks in as far as possible.

Musical Activities

Music can be used in a variety of ways to encourage children to communicate. Most children find some form of music nonthreatening, enjoyable, and even soothing. Relaxing with music often leads to enhanced communication. Use these musical activities to determine a child's preferences, promote language learning, and enhance communication skills.

- Provide a variety of musical instruments and demonstrate how to use them.

- Encourage a child to try to hum or whistle to music.

- Play relaxing music at bedtime, nap time, and rest time.

- Use music that reinforces basic concepts, such as simple counting or color songs.

- Sing songs to indicate transitions. For example, find or make up a "Hello Song," "Clean Up Song," "Goodbye Song," and others.

- Use or make up songs that emphasize following directions and involve movement, such as "Hokey-Pokey."

- Demonstrate cause and effect with music boxes.

- Snap, clap, dance, and rock to music, and encourage child to imitate.

- Expose children to all types of music.

- Allow children to control the music they hear. For example, attach a tape player to a wheelchair so the child can decide when to turn it on and off.

- Sing songs related to special occasions, such as holidays and birthdays.

- Make up and sing songs about what you are doing.

- Help children learn nursery rhymes.

- Give children a variety of instruments to have a parade.

- Sing songs with phrases that repeat, such as "Monkeys in the Bed."

- Sing songs with anticipated parts such as "Pop Goes the Weasel."

- Use rhythm and music to help children remember important information. This can be as simple as the child's name, age, and gender.

- Use songs with children that are fun and upbeat. Incorporate related motions. Suitable favorites include:

  - Head, Shoulders, Knees, and Toes
  - Itsy Bitsy Spider
  - Three Little Fishies
  - Baby Bumblebee
  - This Old Man
  - B-I-N-G-O
  - It's Raining, It's Pouring
  - Hot Cross Buns
  - I'm a Little Teapot
  - I've Been Working on the Railroad
  - This Is the Way We...
  - Mary Had a Little Lamb
  - The Green Grass Grew All Around
  - Twinkle, Twinkle Little Star
  - John Jacob Jingleheimer Schmidt
  - Rock-a-Bye Baby
  - Old MacDonald
  - Wheels on the Bus
  - If You're Happy and You Know It
  - Row, Row, Row Your Boat
  - Hush Little Baby
  - Mulberry Bush
  - The Alphabet Song
  - Muffin Man
  - One, Two, Buckle My Shoe
  - Rain, Rain, Go Away
  - Looby Loo
  - Little Bunny Foo Foo
  - Little Cabin in the Woods
  - Where Has My Little Dog Gone?
  - Frérè Jacques (Are You Sleeping?)
  - The Farmer in the Dell

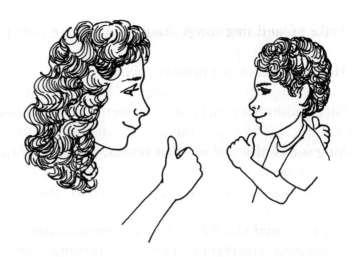

Games

Games provide an enjoyable and nonthreatening framework for developing interactive skills. Most games involve turn-taking, following instructions, repetition, listening, and reacting. Here are some favorites that can easily be adapted to many learning styles and ability levels.

- Pat-a-Cake
- Peek-a-Boo
- "Where" games
- I Spy
- I'm Gonna Get You
- Simon Says
- Red Light, Green Light
- Whisper Down the Lane
- Hide and Seek
- Catch
- Hokey-Pokey
- Ring around the Rosy
- Rough and tumble play (often stimulates communication, but will depend on the child's preferences)
- Duck, Duck, Goose
- London Bridge
- Go Fish (can be adapted to matching colors or other activities on a child's level)
- Memory
- Hot Potato
- Musical Chairs (circles or other marked areas can be used instead of chairs for wheelchair accessibility)
- What's Missing? (display several objects, then remove one and ask the child to try to remember the name of each one)

- The Farmer in the Dell
- Follow the Leader
- This Little Piggy
- Fingerplays (for example, "Where is Thumbkin?" or "Here's the Church")

Invent a game by repeating any action that has made children smile or laugh. Make its occurrence contingent on their indicating they want "more" through eye contact, gesture, or vocalization.

These songs give early interventionists and parents a starting point when planning games for young children. All do not require children to vocalize, but they do all promote interaction and engagement and provide enjoyable experiences to encourage children to communicate.

Activities for Preschoolers

Generally, children become more interested in their peers and display increasingly sophisticated play and verbal skills during their preschool years. During this period of growth, children present a diversity of needs, interests, and abilities. Below is a potpourri of ideas for activities for preschoolers. These activities can and should be adapted to meet the individual needs of children.

- Place room decorations at the child's eye level.

- Display children's artwork.

- Correct inappropriate behavior, such as grabbing toys. Encourage the child to use words instead.

- Reinforce appropriate social behaviors, such as sharing, by calling attention to the behavior with praise.

- Sometimes let a child be the "teacher."

- Encourage children to tell their own names when someone asks.

- Let a child deliver a simple message to someone.

- Introduce the concept of "if...then." For example, say, "If you're tired, then take a nap," or "If you're finished, then put it away."

- Tell children "secrets;" encourage them to tell you some of their own secrets.

- Let children guess the number of objects you have in a jar. Then, pull the objects out of the jar and count them together, one at a time.

- Help a child to play a simple joke or harmless prank on another caregiver.

- Conduct "Show-'n'-Tell," helping children find the appropriate words and providing cues if they are unsure of what to say.

- Discourage "baby talk" when it is no longer appropriate.

- Provide verbal encouragement when a child attempts difficult tasks.

- Help children learn nursery rhymes by reciting them often.

- Use thematic units instead of working on skills in isolation. Theme-related activites provide continuity and pique and maintain children's interest.

- Teach children how to ask others to play by helping them select and approach partners for activities.

- Introduce number concepts by counting fingers, toes, children, and objects.

- Encourage imaginative play by allowing children to use objects for new or "silly" purposes.

- During play or simple experiments, encourage children to predict what will happen.

- Help children differentiate male and female.

- Work on categorization by sorting objects into piles with labels, such as Food and Toys.

- Show children a picture or set of pictures and encourage them to make up a story to go with the pictures.

- Encourage children to ask questions by responding quickly and appropriately when they ask them.

- Allow children to help "cook" or prepare simple snacks to learn sequencing events and activities.

- Help children plan what to do during unstructured times, allow them to follow through with the activity, and later ask them to describe what they did.

- Use mixed age and ability groupings.

- Talk to children, not "over" or about them as if they were not present.

- Help children recount activities experienced in your absence; provide cues if necessary.

- Help children recognize and respond to absurdities by pointing them out in pictures or creating silly situations.

- Give children props and allow them to put them in order as you read a story or sing a song, such as "There Was an Old Lady Who Swallowed a Fly." This helps them learn to sequence objects and events.

- Name and/or show children pictures of objects, then ask them to fetch the real items.

- When asked questions about disabilities, answer them honestly but appropriately for both children and others.

- Prepare children for an imaginary trip by helping them list what they would need to take. For example, if they pretend to go on a picnic, tell what they might like to eat.

- Make a game of displaying a few objects, the taking one away, and having the child guess what is missing.

- Put an object in a box and ask children to tell what it is without looking – only by feeling or shaking it.

- After significant accomplishments, teach children to "pat themselves on the back" and say, "Good for me!"

- Allow both girls and boys to play with all types of toys.

- Encourage expressions of individuality.

- Hold a tea party.

- Encourage children to talk about and label pictures and other creations they make.

- Plan special events, such as parties and field trips.

- Design enticing areas for dramatic play; change them frequently. Examples include a house, a grocery store, and a dress-up trunk with a mirror.

Outings

Although it may not always be convenient, it is important to include children with disabilities in everyday errands and special outings. Participation in these events provides the necessary background for increasingly abstract verbal skills. Upcoming language demands that will incorporate these abstract verbal skills include retelling experiences, categorization, sequencing, and answering questions about what, where, and why activities take place. The number of possible outings is limited only by your imagination, but here are a few ideas of activities and places to go:

- Beach
- Mountains
- Museums
- Activity centers, such as restaurants and other commercial enterprises that specialize in children's parties and related events
- Camping
- Fishing
- Toy stores
- Clothing stores
- Grocery stores
- Church, Sunday school
- Amusement parks
- Riding a bike or tricycle
- Hairdresser and barber
- Parent's workplace
- A friend's house
- Nature walks
- Library
- Laundromat
- Police and fire stations
- Zoo
- Gas stations

- Restaurants (let the child order; some restaurants may have picture menus)
- Theaters
- Circus
- Hotels and motels
- Shopping malls
- Parks
- Fairs
- Playgrounds
- Hospital to visit a sick friend
- Nursing home to visit an elderly friend or family member
- Around the neighborhood to play with other babies and young children
- Concerts
- Games and sporting events
- Ice cream store
- Farm or petting zoo
- Boat, train, or bus ride
- Aquarium
- Country or city (depending on area where child lives)
- Car wash
- Orchards or commercial gardens
- Picnics
- Airport
- Sibling's school
- Pet store
- Bank
- Hayrides, tree festivals, and other seasonal events
- Post office
- Swimming pool
- Long-distance, planned vacations
- Any place the child is invited and can safely attend (try to avoid being overprotective based only on a child's disability; this can prevent participation in valuable learning experiences)

While doing errands, talk about the purpose and the process of what you are doing. For example, say, "We need to mail this letter. First, we must go to the post office to buy stamps, and then we can put the letter in the mailbox." For special events and errands, talk about where you plan to go, why, and what you need to do to prepare for the trip. You might say, "We are going to the beach to visit Grandma. We need to pack our bathing suits so we can go swimming. Then, we will put gas in the car and be ready to go."

Although young children may not understand all of what you say, getting in the habit of providing explanations and language models at all appropriate times is a good idea. Outings are a perfect opportunity to practice this skill.

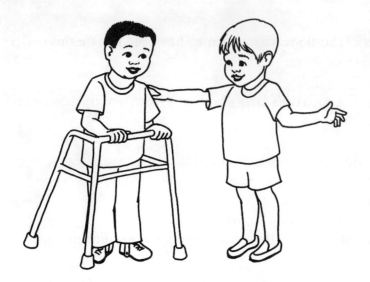

Children with Disabilities

Most of this book is intended for use with children who have any type of disability or developmental delay. Previous suggestions are general enough to be easily adapted to a variety of situations. However, the following considerations should be kept in mind when working with children with the specific conditions listed below.

Physical Disabilities

- Use toys with switches to afford the child maximum independence and to help develop knowledge of cause and effect.

- Take the child shopping, to playgrounds and restaurants, and other places so they will have as much to talk about as their nondisabled peers.

- Allow children to experience the feelings of being over, under, in, out, on top of, and upside down, even when associated activities require physical assistance.

- Keep your expectations high because physical limitations do not lead necessarily to communication delays.

- Talk about the names and functions of any special equipment used, such as braces, wheelchairs, or walkers.

Visual Impairments

- Be sure to provide adequate visual stimulation, regardless of the severity of a child's visual impairment.

- Talk about objects and activities while a child is physically involved with them rather than when the objects or activities first come into view.

- Place children on a child-safe area of the floor where they will receive feedback from a variety of sounds and textures as they explore.

- Realize that, rather than attending to a speaker's face, children with visual impairments often turn an ear toward the speaker's voice.

- Keep in mind that many children with visual impairments may not enjoy being tossed, swung, thrown in the air, or bounced because they may not receive the visual feedback that often provides security and orientation during such activities.

- Select toys that combine auditory and tactile elements with intense visual stimulation.

Health Conditions

- Stabilization of any medical conditions is the first priority with any child. Explaining necessary medical procedures in simple terms as they are happening is important.

- Remember many of a child's early words may be related to medical equipment, supplies, or procedures.

- Allow a child to have as many firsthand experiences with other children and different environments as physicians permit.

- Expose children to activities in which they cannot participate directly by using videos, books, and conversations.

Hearing Impairments

- Be certain children are looking at you when you speak.

- Make sure children wear their hearing aids at all times except when they are sleeping.

- Always speak while signing, regardless of a child's hearing ability.

- Encourage children to vocalize while signing.

- Read to children, using related signs, exaggerate facial expressions, and vary vocal tone. Make sure they can see the pictures and text as you read. Pair the directions you give with appropriate gestures.

- Work in close collaboration with an audiologist or speech-language pathologist.

Related Readings

Bricker, D. and Cripe, J. *An activity-based approach to early intervention.* Baltimore: Paul H. Brookes, 1992.

Hart, B. and Risley, T.R. *Meaningful differences in the everyday experiences of young American children.* Baltimore: Paul H. Brookes, 1995.

Kaiser, A.P. and Gray, D.B. *Enhancing children's communication: Research foundations for intervention.* Baltimore: Paul H. Brookes, 1993.